THE RESURRECTION TRADE

THE RESURRECTION TRADE

poems by

Leslie Adrienne Miller

Graywolf Press

SAINT PAUL, MINNESOTA

Publication of this volume is made possible in part by a grant provided by the Minnesota State Arts Board, through an appropriation by the Minnesota State Legislature; a grant from the Wells Fargo Foundation Minnesota; and a grant from the National Endowment for the Arts, which believes that a great nation deserves great art. Significant support has also been provided by the Bush Foundation; Target; the McKnight Foundation; and other generous contributions from foundations, corporations, and individuals. To these organizations and individuals we offer our heartfelt thanks.

Published by Graywolf Press
2402 University Avenue, Suite 203
Saint Paul, Minnesota 55114
All rights reserved.

www.graywolfpress.org

Published in the United States of America

ISBN-13: 978-1-55597-463-3
ISBN-10: 1-55597-463-5

2 4 6 8 9 7 5 3 1
First Graywolf Printing, 2007

Library of Congress Control Number: 2006929503

Cover design: Kyle G. Hunter

Cover art: Jacques Fabien Gautier D'Agoty, *Anatomie des parties de la génération de l'homme et de la femme,* Paris, 1773. Colored mezzotint. National Library of Medicine, National Institutes of Health

ACKNOWLEDGMENTS

Grateful acknowledgment is made to the editorial staff of the following publications in which these poems first appeared.

The Antioch Review: "Sonnet on the Interval During Which the Sun Is Below the Horizon at an Angle Less than Any of Several Standard Angular Distances"

Big Muddy: *Mississippi Journal*: "Easter Flood"

City Pages: "The Harriers"

Climate Controlled: "Hydrologic Sonnet"

Great River Review: "Up North," "Bridge Club," "Bridal Wear," "Mother and Son," "Mimosa"

The Kenyon Review: "Wandering Uterus," "Aim"

Luna: "Homage to a Testore Bass"

Nimrod International Journal of Poetry & Prose: "Parous in Paris," "Map of the Interior," "Torso of a Woman Gone with Child, 1774"

North American Review: "Pregnant in Florence"

North Dakota Quarterly: "Motherhood as Place," "Speaking of the Devil," "Shopping for the Queen of England"

North Stone Review: "Subtitles," "*Plastic Cultura, Andalucía,*" "The Dead Send Their Gardener"

Ploughshares: "Étude"

Poems & Plays 7: "Outliving the Lyric Moment"

Prairie Schooner: "Madame du Coudray's Woman Machine, 1756," "Gautier D'Agoty's Écorchés," "Mirabilia, 1726"

Southern Indiana Review: "Hydrologic Sonnet"

Willow Springs: "Mantra of the Bath" (under the title "The Turtle of Love"), "Weaning"

The author wishes to thank *Fundación Valparaíso,* Almería, Spain; *Le Château de Lavigny Maison d'écrivains,* Foundation Ledig–Rowohlt, Switzerland; and the Anderson Center, Red Wing, Minnesota, for invaluable residencies during which many of these poems were composed. I also wish to thank my colleagues at the University of Saint Thomas for grants and course releases that allowed me time to finish this work.

CONTENTS

for Sebastian Dante Williamson who led the way

There is a mind in the flesh. A mind as quick as lightning.

Antonin Artaud
Art and Death

I always said God was against art and I still believe it.

Edward Elgar
in a letter to a friend after the
unsuccessful premiere of *Gerontius*

THE RESURRECTION TRADE

ÉTUDE

All my life before him, every word I wrote
had heard the notes turning into air above the pages
and spinning my desire into jail and joy,
or memory of someone not quite gone.
Like children in the womb or eggs asleep
in a girl's all possible, the words I gave to paper
heard whatever I heard and bore the residue
of Janáçek and Liszt, Grieg and Shostakovich.
But when I met the man I'd marry, he gave me
names for what I'd always loved without a word,
and played his bass beneath, beside and over me,
so I began to listen differently, the symphonies
that once had slipped so easily beneath the page,
suddenly a competition, and every day I turned
the volume down a little more until there was
this silence, these white pages that I offer you,
written without music. Except for the cry
of my child.

GAUTIER D'AGOTY'S ÉCORCHÉS

Anatomie des parties de la génération, Paris, 1773

What have they done to deserve this beauty?
Did they, like Marsyas, invite some knife-
wielding god with petty transgressions,
the crime of a few tunes on Athena's lost flute?

Or were they simply too poor for deep
graves, locked gates, and good husbands
to watch over the mounds of new soil
tossed toward them and their hunted unborn?

Whoever they were, they're still with us,
posing demurely in suits of blood
and muscle, the bruised shadows
of what skin they do have, purpling like

crushed petunias as they spread their legs
and raise their meaty arms to show
dissected breasts, unfinished infants, sundry
viscera on the ground about their feet

as if this were Thanksgiving and they
cornucopias stuffed with squash and fruit.
And who delivered their sentences?
Surely not the muses who, at least,

let them keep rococo faces. In 1773
the womb and brain were the last outposts
of the body to be mapped. D'Agoty bought
the rights to Le Blon's technique of printing

mezzotints and gave these ladies homes
in scientific texts, but anatomists believed
D'Agoty's prints too gorgeous to be accurate.
Perhaps that's why they open other wounds

so easily in us. All so like the single rabbit
I downed at twenty with a borrowed rifle,
and then was obligated to see skinned,
first a scoring the length of the spine,

then the peeling of the fur in one steaming piece,
while the perverse uncle who clearly desired
to touch me, instead held up a dripping pelt
in one hand, and in the other, a flayed carcass

still wrapped in its bundle of muscle like a gift.

ROUGH MUSIC, EDINBURGH, 1829

Why shouldn't Dr. Knox have invited
his painter friend to view the body
of the girl he knew was too fresh
for legitimate death, her "handsome"
limbs and alabaster waist a crime
to cut before at least one brush
could render her unscathed on paper?
Had she been any less an odalisque,
perhaps he wouldn't have needed to collude
with artists or waste good whiskey
to keep the cream in her hips, her purpled
lips all the more arresting than they'd been
in life. If he'd found her sooner and living
would he have known all this was there
for purchase? Would he have offered
to keep her in dresses and tea for peeks?
In the weeks after Hare had turned
King's evidence on Burke and the latter's
convicted corpse was flayed and offered up
to forty thousand pairs of public eyes,
Knox refused to speak. Though by report
she'd been delivered to Surgeons Square
still warm and clutching twopence-halfpenny
someone paid to bed her, they cut her hair
before she cooled, and Mary swam three
months in whiskey before they took her skin
apart to look inside. When the story broke,
an angry mob came after Knox with noise,
an opera of whistles, pots and pans,

and tore his effigy to shreds in Newington
outside his house. And if in Mary Paterson
a child had taken root, no one would be the wiser
if Knox had kept the little lyric of it to himself,
scion fathered by the Scottish city's lust,
gift to men of science, and so also to me,
woman of the new world digging through
old books to resurrect her murdered parts,
to offer her my own rough music, the strange
collusion of imaginary science and real art.

MOTHER AND SON

The night after the twin towers evaporated in jet fuel
and dust, my nephew asked my sister to stand up

beside his bed, her arms down tight along her hips.
He was clear about how he wanted her, straight, tall,

as rigid as possible. He'd said his prayers, read
his bedtime story of a girl with golden hair locked

in a stairless tower by a witch whose motives weren't
entirely clear. He'd seen the footage at school that day,

heard the talk meant to help him "process," and yet,
he couldn't help himself: he had to ask his mother

to put her body up. Exactly one year since her diagnosis,
the rounds of chemo, her lost and rebuilt breasts, months

of fighting the port beneath her rib, hats and wigs,
pallor, fear and end to her childbearing years.

He'd seen it all under cover of blouses and pads, taken
then made again, breast from which he'd fed, chest

he'd fallen to sleep against all his seven years.
My sister obeyed her son and stood upright

beside his bed, heeded his command to close her eyes,
then heard his *eeeeeewww, crash* and felt the lump

of processed fur that was his teddy bear
hit her shoulder right about the 95th floor, or where

her good breast stood beside its remade twin: 3,000 deaths
he wouldn't understand against the one he might.

Fascinated with logistics, he's made his LEGOs
tell this story as well as television or the anger

of his father at the screen. The child must have thought
towers come down more easily than mothers, but now

he sees how both bodies and buildings offer up their undefended
heights. He giggles at his mother's startled stammer of his name

with, is it reprimand or sorrow? This is what he'd wished
to learn: whether to be sad or mad, but his mother

doesn't know herself. In tears, she takes the downed bear
and bewildered boy in her arms, and hugs them and hugs them

against the changed landscape of her womanhood.

WANDERING UTERUS

Leonardo believed that semen came down
from the brain through a channel in the spine.

And that female lactation held its kick off
in the uterus. Not as bad as Hippocrates

who thought the womb wandered the ruddy
crags of a woman's body, wreaking a havoc

whenever it lodged, shoving aside
more sensible organs like the heart.

All manner of moral failings, snits
and panics were thus explained, the wayward

organ floating like Cleopatra's barge
down the murky canal of any appendage

or tying up at the bog of the throat.
One can't help but imagine a little halved

walnut of a boat like that in Leonardo's
drawing, the curled meat of the fetus

tucked inside, harboring near a naughty eye
or rebellious ear that never can hear

what a man might mean when he says *yes*
or *always*. It's all still beautifully true

what these good scientists alleged: the brain
is as good a place as any for the manufacture

of evanescence, and why not allow
that the round and sturdy skiff of the uterus

may float and flaunt its special appetite for novelty,
even if we dub it dumb, lined with tentacles,

many chambered, and errant as the proverbial knight
seeking out adventure, but loyal to one queen.

TO MAKE A WOUND

Better than the howl of the dog whose fur punishes
the throat, better than the leathery rind of mother
whose simple loud "ouch" doesn't thrill, the biter
wants the scream attached to the softness, his jaws
electrified by the give of foamy baby skin.

He can't resist the cheek that speaks of sea
spray, tastes of fleece, milk and pearl.
He hasn't even discovered my boy's
chubby toes and soft hip handles,
his creamy bracelets of pulp.

It's the glare of new cheek that invites teeth,
and the biter leans toward it, mouth open,
closing his eyes like a girl about to enter
her first undoing. My bitten son, in turn,
learns to bite me too, opens his kitten maw

on my shoulders and nipples, wrists and calves
with their branches of tendon and muscle,
whatever he finds bare and moist
as the meat of the yellow pears he craves.
How can he be expected to know meal

from blossom, flesh from flower? The wind tickles
his lips, and his eyes fix on the pale places
that might be food or opportunity to wound.
One day his biter buddy will nibble
the unlit coin of flesh beneath his lover's nape,

and he'll remember my son's meringue,
though the time and place of the taste will have vanished,
leaving only a whiff of sweet white that cries out
to be marked. The biter's a pretty boy
with dusky eyes and a wren-like mother

in a red suit and clicking heels. When he bites,
he's banished again from hugs and touch, and a hunger
burgeons in his knit brow that lovers will crave
in twenty years, and to which they'll offer their girly
spume and cream. And in each offering perhaps

another tiny jaw will etch itself in the womb
of a woman whose lover has held the taste
of my son's skin on his tongue for years,
certain there would be something else
in the world that aches for the mark of his pleasure,

that pays with this exquisite sip of flesh.

THE DEATH OF IRONY

My eye first caught him in the neighbor's birdbath,
an enormous shimmering right down to his rolling
eye, the white of it the only gap in all that sleek black.
Sick, wounded, but upright and regal in the stone bowl,
he watched across the fence as I tossed a ball
to my two year old, and it came to me
that nothing with wings should sit still that long.
When I went over, he flapped the feeble fan
of his right wing and dragged one clenched claw
over the lip of the stone, so I saw there was more
than a simple broken part. His glossy neck bristled,
and he glared at me before he lost his grip and fell.
Had he been a swallow or even a robin, I'd have shoveled
him into the alley on the spot, but he was like some movie
of a bird, something intimate I'd never see so close again,
only feel in the broad shadows and cackles
of his kin falling over the neighborhood.
So I took him a scoop of chicken feed, poured it
over his beak as he rolled one eye in warning,
and I took my child indoors straightaway,
thinking of how whatever it was that had downed
that creature would bloom in the drops sucked
from his prone corpse in the sun all day,
and fly in the night over and into the bodies
of everyone I love. Still alive at dawn
when I came again to see what could be done,
his neck greasy and bare where some cat
had taken its turn, he gazed at me once more

before the spade came down on his head,
but I was already elsewhere, thinking of how
my husband's ex announced she'd dreamed
about my son. How like her own he seemed.

SPEAKING OF THE DEVIL

Just when I begin to believe English is lucky,
full of choices like *trumpet* and *ash*, *curlicue*,
olive, *armrest* and *hostile*, I see that its vastness

is urban, lonely: too many people live in its center,
and the environs are losing population fast.
Few are interested in leaving the inner cities of language,

so each tongue shrinks, deletes its consummate
geographies, *copse* and *dell*, *ravine* and *fen*,
boonies, *coulées*, *bailiwicks*, and *sloughs*.

But English is not the only shrinking province.
I watch two French boys on the train
from Turin to Nice burn a pair of earphones,

delighted as the plastic withers, whitens,
sends up its little wick of toxic smoke. *Watch*
and *wow* and *fuck,* all the words they need to test

the butane's power to make plastic disappear.
Not sure if I can understand their chat, they test me too.
The one with his thumb on the flame looks at me

from under lavish lashes, merest shadow
of mustache riding his budded lips, *Diable*,
he asks me, *how you say him in English?*

and I marvel at how few syllables
anyone needs to make a world.

MIMOSA

She writes that her mimosa is in bloom in Rome
and goes so far as to imagine that it might match
the yellow room of my infant son. There is hard talk
of war and a feeling between us that my country
is much in the wrong. She reads her newspapers

in Rome and I the local rag, but the stories we get
are different, the fears rising along the spines
of our thought fueled by our own what-is-at-hand.
The little pom-poms of her mimosa are more brilliant
to my mind than the vials Iraq denies,

and the yellow walls of my boy's dreams
have been with her as long as this threat
of war. Do we imagine these delicate things
because of the threat? Or is our minds' small
produce antidote? Beauty is already obsolete

in art, so the mystery of mimosa on the breeze
is moot. And anyhow the tree she means
isn't the American variety bearing frizzy
blossoms, floozy and pink, but Europe's
sturdy gold acacia. Not until I'd spent

a spring in France and seen the yellow bombs
go off in all the woods did I understand
those Dutch still lifes with fistfuls of mimosa
in tankards beside opened melons and gutted rabbits,
or read my friend's words and see

as she did. But the war of which she speaks
gropes on in the periphery of my unknowing—
a sentience of wholly plastic depictions.
Only once in my life have I even seen a freshly
dead body, a woman on a highway

in the Andalusian desert. My bus happened
on that road only moments after the collision;
and beyond the obvious blood, there was a man
also bloody in the road, holding a limp woman
in his arms. It was not the open skull or broken

car that hissed at us, but the way the living
partner's body keened. The boy in the yellow nursery
is my only child, born to me late in life. He'll be
blond, white, male and Christian in a world where
others aren't, so peril hangs above him like the four

pastel animals of the mobile we had to remove
when he sat up, touched them and understood
they could be brought down. For months
they'd circled above him, a vision of delicacy singing
their one song, and while he watched them churning

in the dark, he stopped the howling we couldn't
interpret, just as I, dark mornings in February
in Provence, woke to the sparks of the one mimosa
on the mountain and believed there was no other
world than the heaven of that tree turning in the sun.

PLASTIC CULTURA, ANDALUCÍA

As we spiral down from the Sierra de Gádor
we know nothing of what will appear below,
expect only the sea at Almería, a bright blue
plate that will fall from the sky and blot with whitecaps.

We've been all day on ribbons of road wrapping crags
from Puerto del Suspiro del Moro through Lanjarón,
Cádiar, Yegen, white villages that shimmer and blind,
terraces of silver olive and yellow almond. We wear eyes

from other places, Copenhagen and Edmonton,
Paris and Saint Paul, so we're ready for only beauty here:
La mer, el mar, the sea. We gasp as pearly pools
appear below and ride the limit of our gaze.

We descend enchanted, hold our breath—then no,
it's not the coast, but lakes of plastic, ghost lagoons.
Synthetic waves lap the road on either side.
The actual sea's much farther than we thought.

Milky with dust, shredded by arid wind
which otherwise would never let the tender vines
of peas and peppers thrive, these fragile tents
drink up the light, stand in for sea. We ride amazed

through rags of flapping plastic and search the open seams
for green. All Europe's winter produce crouches in giant bags,
eggplants, lilies, lettuce holding fast in sand and muck,
fed its steady drip of toxins in mock rain. At last

we pass it, relieved to find the road can climb again
flinty and pale toward Turre and Mojácar, barren crags
where we'll be thankful guests, sit down to our green meal
and never wonder who must answer for our hunger.

MAP OF THE INTERIOR

a mostly found poem

Vesalius has failed to give his name
to any anatomical part. In this
he differs from intrepid others
who found it de rigueur to map
with pen and paper after they'd applied
the knife. Hence we have the airway
of Eustachius, the tube of Fallopius,
the duct of Botallus, the circle
of Willis, the lobe of Spigelius,
the fissure of Sylvius, the glands
of Bartholin, the island of Reil,
the ganglion of Gasser, the cartilage
of Arantius, the sinus of Valsalva,
the tubercle of Lower, the valves
of Morgagni, the torcular of Herophilus
the veins of Galen, and the alleged
spot of Grafenberg.

ON THE VULVA

figure 1

Though the actual drawing is carefully excised
from my venerable university library's copy

(Did the censor stumble on her by accident?
Or was she part of some purposeful purge?),

I can imagine her be-muscled thighs cocked
and open on the halved fruit of the vulva.

After all, I've done my time under paper sheets
looking up at photographs like this in color stills.

But Leonardo's text is still intact, and *castle*
makes me laugh, applied, as one could never guess

to what lies beyond the open door of the absent
figure's spread legs, and better yet, *gate-keeper*

seems to indicate the missing clitoris
riding its long wrinkle of inert flesh.

Leonardo did his best to show us what he knew,
even if anatomists of centuries much closer

to our own judged her much more cruelly.
See Dickinson's catalogue of unkind notes:

Age 37, 2 children . . . pallid and glazed (fig. 84)
(No righteous bowdlerizer here),

Old hypertrophies in stout woman (fig. 93),
or this from *figure 98, Flexible glue mold*

of tear in labor, for student repair,
and *figure 99*, a whole page of *Hymens*

stretched, nicked, worn and gone.
Ditto *100, All life size*, mind you, one poor

smashed pomegranate labeled *Husband and wife*
both complain of her wide opening.

The *male meatus* fares a little better
with happier notes like *after hot bath (111),*

prow type (112), and *Penis made*
of sealing wax for woman's self relief (114 a).

figure 99

Inordinate sex curious-
ity; 15 lovers before
marriage at 21.
Powerful husband,
30-60 minutes, 4 to
7 times a week, she
4-7 orgasms, maxi-
mum 12. Three
children. One
boy lover 2¼
diameter, ditto
champion
prize fighter.
Her entroitus 2¼
Able woman.

RECIPE FOR COUPLES THERAPY

Would that my husband had read Hippocrates'
Nature of Women, especially that bit
about the "Dislocation of the womb."
Who knows what sets it off, the poor old
tire deflated by some entirely benign
remark. Happens all the time to those of us
in late middle age. I myself can't even
count the number of times my parts
have gone over to the liver in the last year—
and then, it's true, my voice is simply
toast, nothing but a muffled sob,
and the dull broken record of one's suffering
scrapes to a stop. Oh, if only we'd had that sweet-
scented wine on hand, or known just what
foul-scented vapors to torch beneath
my shorts. Eventually, Hippocrates believed,
pregnancy would cure such naughty
waftings in the groin, but it didn't work for me.

And then there's the real zinger: when the womb
heads for the hips! You'll know it when you see,
he says, the mouth of the womb turned to the hip,
and then it gets complicated, involving all kinds
of things that are pretty hard to locate,
undiluted sheep's milk, fennel and absinthe
right where the panty hamster smiles. Then
you've got to find squills, opium poppies, and rose
perfume (easy enough), four cantharid beetles
with their legs, wings and heads removed

(poor things), four dark peony seeds, cuttlefish
eggs, and a little parsley seed in wine.
And when you finally start to bleed, he advises,
live it up gal, get it on with your man,
and be sure to eat some boiled squid.

BRIDGE CLUB

It comes back to me as a tangled after-dark cackle,
female, roughed up by cigarettes and scotch,
wakes me into the possibility that something
is being missed. A fleet of card tables set up

across three rooms, an armada of liquor bottles
lining the kitchen, mother cooking the "company"
dish out of a book. My sister and I, bathed,
pajamaed, are handled, smeared with scent

and coo by the ladies, teased and pinched by the men.
Father presides over vodka, gin, rusty Manhattan mix,
a shaker with cartoons of busty ladies toasting mirth.
After *I Dream of Jeannie* and *Gunsmoke* I'm put down

in my bunk which shares a wall with the party,
so I wake each hour hearing the laughter turn,
fill with silliness and edge: tatters of gossip
doused in the toilet's incessant flush.

Deep in the furry hide of my childhood, I listen
and steal bits of story, dream of my play,
captured lizards and mud huts, graves
for cats and unweaned rabbits. Smoke, whisper,

booze and great pans of mother's mushroom chicken
in wine disappearing in riffs of chatter and flashes of flesh
in among Jeannie's sequins and veils. The mocking snicker
and purr of *Oh Master* merged with the same sound

from one of mother's friends. But which one?
My mother is Miss Kitty following the drunks
with her sponge, lifting stains of sauce and ash.
Horse tails, trolls, and the satin settee in Jeannie's bottle

all fall into the laughter of one stalled woman,
flirty, high and tight, forced out in little bursts
of derailed wit, the bitter snigger of a woman
who must have felt judged by a mother like mine.

And now the memory of that laughter is another mother,
the only one who had a body. I hold on to her single
wrong note and know it's a gift. She had a good husband
on whom she would cheat, and who also would die young,

so her eldest girl would hold the loss against her for good.
But me, I remember the plush bundle of her breasts
bathed in perfume, the zeros of smoke that issued
from her slickered lips, her raw blonde mane,

her *honey* and blood talk, she who educated
the whole neighborhood about sex and power.
She who knew the world we were headed for
in no way resembled the one we'd been promised.

VENUS ENDORMI

and her four instructive sisters

Collection anatomique Spitzner
Musée Orfila, Paris

Professeur Delmas agrees to demonstrate
his bevy of waxwork models under glass,
the first, endearing *Venus Endormi,*
the only purely decorative one, sleeps
and breathes at the flip of a switch,
her chest gauzed with a smocked
Parisian gown through which
pretty nipples throb up at us
with each surge of a wheezing
antique pump. The other four
are built to educate, all awake,
and equally demurely gowned.
Normale lolls in a nest of borrowed
tresses, dark as the lender's final hour,
while *Forceps* sports a spray of slotted spoons,
and *Le Crochet* a bouquet of hooks.
But *La Césarienne* is filleted, a fringe
of disembodied fingers arrayed
along the cut, wherein the shiny coil
of her never-born naps on, serene,
ready to be lifted toward the mocking
O of mother's cartoon scream.

SUBTITLES

Lakes of blue light, jowl shadows, black leather jackets,
women with pert noses and small Joan of Arc jaws.
Furious smoking. The problem is always *feeling*:
gradations of disconsolance, not quite grief,
but enigmatic waves of near sentiment spilled.
A dozen people getting on and off trains.
Rhythmic shouting, long sad looks, hair tossing,
a car crumpled in a wheat field, and a man weeping.
Why is this grim anterior so compelling
that I hunch close to the screen, swallow the yellow titles
greedily, drink up that world of cramped spaces, rain,
and meaningful looks as if it were abundant cheap wine?
Nostalgia? The bleak and encyclopedic mysteries
of Europe — an addiction? Tolstoy's locomotives,
Hugo's brutal hungers. Werther's ridiculous
sorrows. I in my bald and lobotomized land
where snow falls on the town and the men go north
to fish through the ice, where meaningful looks mar
the linear plots, and marriages go down like tiny planes
in the ten thousand lakes the state boasts.

SHOPPING FOR THE QUEEN OF ENGLAND

Today in The Bead Monkey, I watch a pack
of seven-year-old girls squealing over trays of fairies
no bigger than their pinky nails, gold and pewter puppies,
tiny boom boxes, tops, a saxophone with all the stops.

Amazing for their details, these miniatures draw
the girl in me as well, and I squander half an hour pawing
through the teensy trinkets with tiny wings,
moving parts: an itty-bitty cheese, tools and bottles,

Lilliputian pots, settees and silver cutlery.
Arranged by theme, the store's no bigger than my kitchen
but full of girls and women with little wooden trays
bagging beads and trifles, crystal, cloisonné,

and malachite, silken thread and every sort
of clasp to capture all these charms. I wouldn't
have come to such a place except my friend
is making a book for the Queen of England,

photographs she shot one afternoon in Oxford
when the Queen alighted from her Rolls
in splendid rainy light that pooled in folds
of her cobalt suit and matching pillbox hat.

Now she searches for the right red bead to close
the cover on her handmade book of thumb-sized queens
to send the royal collection, and I, along for the ride,
am struck again with waves of admiration

for my friend's ability to arrange a room, a life,
a book fitting for a queen. In the disarray
and grit of days with man and children, I've forgotten
what it is to frame some small ethereal spot

like a clear high note or the precise shock
of one red silk throw in a room of twenty blues—
so I'm seized with this impossible mix of love
and envy for my friend who still maintains the palace

of a single woman, who still believes that men
like our fathers will arrive and admire her archival
skill, her knowledge of exactly what each hue
and weave articulate, who still believes a man

will want her for, and not in spite of, this gift.
But I know her beaus will wish for larger, uglier
chairs, rifled magazines on all the tables. I walk
her dustless rooms enchanted by translucent swaths

and dried blooms, every useless, pretty dish.
I see each tassel and stitch the way she means
it to be seen, so I don't need to wonder when we
shoulder in among the birthday party girls,

why they all adore these gilded charms, why each trills
with satisfaction when she finds the perfect flourish,
precious enough to fancy, tiny enough to adorn
the arches of her bare and most enticing parts.

THE DEAD SEND THEIR GARDENER

He arrives in the courtyard with two cartons
of juice, each of which he'll tip and drain
at one go in the heat, and a sack of food
for the roses. He looms over his tools,
blond and dusty as a stalk of ripe wheat,
surely someone's prized lover. Centuries
bask among his hybrid teas, and he shakes
his capable handfuls of food into their beds
until nothing but roses nose the blues between lake
and garden, lake and sky, the lapse of lawn
where a party could be if those who lived here once
returned to pour the wine. She'd be the sort
to tuck a bud behind her ear, and he to catch
one in his teeth. But alas, we're guests
of the present, expectant and sultry; all
graciousness is fled, and rain fills the spent
blooms, tumbles their tops, weighted with ruffles
and shocks of pink. The gardener too disappears
with his breeches the color of mustard and cinched
with a string, gone back into the pages of Hardy
or Lawrence. Perhaps, he'll appear again Tuesday next,
but he won't look any of us living in the eye.

THE RESURRECTION TRADE

on Gautier D'Agoty's Anatomie des parties
de la génération, Paris, 1773

Only the dead are without fear.
— Mexican Villager, *The Magnificent Seven*

Pl. I

A man, his clean skull atop a whole clockwork
of tiny pipes, rigging and marbled meat, one arm
and shoulder stripped of skin. The penis
unjacketed but intact.

Plan. II

His legs alone. Pelvis and organs of generation
scattered about his feet. Also (*fig 5*) a cup?
a wine glass? Something, certainly, in which to catch
the pearly stuff. One leg peeled clean,
the other a river of wire.

Plan. III

She entire, arm raised, profiled looking left,
unwrapped entirely of skin except for two
breasts, neck and one greeny cream of shoulder.

Planche IV

Her bottom half and Dagoty's tidy note:
Dissequée Peint et Gravé par Gautier Dagoty Pere 1773.

Pelvis at her feet, yellow gold
and sturdy as a tavern chair, sockets
and leg bones polished with blue,
the curved wings of the pelvic bones
hovering over the slot where the child
would rest. Bones clearly the least
perturbable blocks of the unbuilt body.

Plan. V

Pregnant now, looking over her flayed shoulder
exquisitely tailored into deltoid epaulette *(A)*,
a sporty trapezius cape *(C)*, and pointy latissimus
dorsi bodice *(B)* inscribed with spiders of inaccurate
veins, face and one perky breast still jacketed in skin.

Coifed, composed in a manner suitable
for rendering in oils, she rests her elbows
on the swell of gray and surely dead *(d)*
infant intent on reading his own fat knees.

Below which: *les parties du Sexe feminine détacheés*
Read: detachable female sex parts

Plan. VI

Her lower body mid-prance, *sans* pelt,
and another whole self
seated and spread-eagled at her feet,
looking at her own knees

as if in echo of the child in utero,
giving us *Le Mont de Vénus (A),*

& (aa) La Plevre, (no longer in the living
language, but lovely like *vulva* or *vagus*).

Here noted also:
>La Femme sur la fin de sa grossesse
>Read: The woman at the end of her grossness

>et la Femme en travail dissequées mortes
>and the woman at work, dissected, dead,

>en cet état et graveés en couleurs
>in state and engraved in colors

par G. Dagoty pere Anatomiste
pensioné du Roi 1773.

Curiosity seldom fails on so grand a scale.
Thus also: *On a donné à ces figures*
>One gives to these figures

>*un air de vie,*
>an air of life, even if *oxygen* (1788)
>doesn't yet exist,

>*pour oter,* to remove,
>*un aspect plus désagréable,*
>the more disagreeable aspect.

She is, after all, a corpse, a cadaver, *cadavre*
      as in, a cadaver has been found in the river.

      How to enter in without extinguishing
      a life. As *Dagoty Pere* reminds on every page
      he passed this art to *fils,* his son, so there had to be
      a she into whom and onto whom he gazed,
      desire etched with purpose other than
      the Lord's. And to what extent did Madame
      live in what her husband read
      in darkness with the wand and nib?
      He who never saw the living
      mother of his son inside out,
      and yet he drew them with his knife.

The child's ear slightly larger than it ought,
doodled veins random from collapse
when air unspiraled from the lungs,
that *air de vie.* And perhaps,
thinking of his own at home,
the artist tried to give it back.

   Plan. VII

Les Extrémités inferieures
(Roughly: inferior boundaries,
or if the literal is preferable, lower half)
the terrible O of her vulva mid-song,

la femme en travail
(Yes, the woman at work!)

>on which the breasts are labeled *tetons,*
>and the curtains on the vulva, *Les Nimphes.*

Wearing a costume of blood
that only art was able to save,
she meets her garish second self again
in this mezzotinted book, opened
like the nipple readied for her child,
on the flannelled knees of those
who could afford these pricey peeps.
Greener than you'd think, so many
filaments scratched into the hair and eyes,
each nameable part lettered by hand.

>*Plan. VIII*
>*Anatomie du Fetus dissequée et gravée*

Looking back, we find the artist knew and copied out a line of Ovid:
Imperfectus adhuc infans genitricis ab alvo.
>Maybe: The infant arrives imperfect from its mother's womb.
>Or the imperfect infant arrives?

Either way,

Too small, the ears grow out of the child's cheeks,
and his eyebrows bush over his open eyes.

The page withers around a tiny yellow hole,
the signature of later, someone's pipe left burning.

The imperfection catalogued and curled by now
in evaporated spirit. What couldn't *arrive*
or what simply didn't, shelved
in the anatomist's vault, wherefrom
the doll-like parts keen to transparent knees,
and gummy fins of fists balled at giant ears
stopper strains of _____
      (*is there any name for sound
      a woman makes contracting?*)
as they float in the firmament
of the Enlightenment's last
human mystery.

TORSO OF A WOMAN GONE WITH CHILD, 1774

Why Jan van Rymsdyck made two versions
of his drawing for Hunter's *Anatomy*
of the human gravid uterus, we can only guess.
The female torso has her dress
peeled upward like her skin, to reveal
the giant egg-shaped uterus
in its nest of shining entrails,
below which a smattering of pubic hair
smudges the upper thighs, and the tops
of her ungartered stockings sag
as if she had just wandered out
of any one of Lautrec's dance hall scenes
and keeled on the spot. More curious still
is the fact that one of Rymsdyck's
drawings has an open book between the thighs,
the slim entrance to the world of this woman's
gravid uterus curtained with a gilt-edged spine,
as if her nether parts were deep in study
of some esoteric subject, as if her reading eyes
were there where her desire once lived.

MADAME DU COUDRAY'S WOMAN MACHINE, 1756

I perfected an invention that pity made me imagine.

—Madame Le Boursier du Coudray, *Abrégé*

After D'Agoty's macabre écorchés
and Rymsdyck's tendency to coil
his innards tight as bags of fists
and then to paint a fatty sheen
on every part, I gasp out loud
when I find Le Boursier's soft machine
of linen and leather, the woman's thighs
great hams of rosy fabric gathered
at the knees like parlor bolsters,
the plush swell of belly draped
in a modest apron opened in a V,
that all who would deliver her
might see the fine embroidery
of the wrinkled vulva giving way
to the crowning cloth doll, one puffed
umbilical cord to announce life,
another flat to advertise a death.
While D'Agoty's sexy écorchés
live on in countless volumes, only one
of Madame du Coudray's *machines*
for instruction in the art of birth
remains, this one with its wicker bones
and wooden pelvis replaces her original
which tucked a gate of real pelvic bones
inside the giant cushion. Sundry detached

pieces lie about: the pillowy placenta
as if infused with waters still, the warning
of a crushed and severed infant skull
to show the damage of an unforgiving tug.
She made her mannequin of cloth
for the women of Clermont who couldn't read,
much less afford D'Agoty's illustrated books,
who worried more about the warming
of the wine and butter in which a living child
was cleansed, or the sturdy shoes the dead
would need for traveling hard dark roads
to nurse their babies from the grave.
She listened while they spoke of prolapse,
mangled parts, torn limbs and broken backs,
the ragged, filthy fingernail of someone's
helpful aunt or neighbor tearing the sight
from a child's eye. From these tales
she fashioned her machine, pushing
her needles through the flesh-colored cloth
as capably as she pushed her hands,
merciful and clean, into the darkened rooms
of a thousand unupholstered wombs.

EASTER FLOOD

Are we sated by the vistas of water,
titillated by the landscape's long scars
of silver, or merely caught unawares
by our thirst for public havoc?
My sister and her husband took their child

and went home from our holiday,
leaving a cramp in the social fabric,
a proximity we'd all tolerated while one feast
laved over into another, and the children
went on inventing their world in the yard

with fairies and sailors and calls
for more stuffing, more cake. Now
the boulevards and avenues open wide
to just us as we drive toward the bluff's
promise of bloody sunset and floodscape,

the risen waters of the Mississippi claiming
the airport, a train yard, warehouse
and small web of woods not yet greened.
The bluffs are full of gawkers taking in
the whole sweep of swallowed valley.

New lakes fill with wind waves.
Electrical stations sandbagged along
the tracks raise their solitary towers,
and the two long hangars of planes
ride out of the drowned land like whales

and arc back into their semblance of sea.
People pour out of cars and into the wind,
whole families released from the close
quarters of Easter with cousins and in-laws,
siblings and parents, pets and dishes,

the stifle of feast upon feast, all seeking
expansive views from the bluffs,
balm of risen vistas of water, the beautiful
and public disaster of flood. They huddle
in the stinging wind beside the city jail

to see the island band shell up to its waist
in waters, the threatened pleasure boats
perched on blocks along the park road.
Chocolate bunnies left headless on tables
all over the city, their torsos gaping

at the necks where children abandoned them
for the promise of bigger calamities. All eyes
gorge themselves on river and river and river.
We come home in the dusk to the deluge
of our own bodies, our homes and beds rife

with the smells of in-laws to whom we gave
them up. We snap out clean bedding, spread
the wafts of cotton like new vistas of water
around the tiny continents of our resurrected
privacies, our recovered intimate distances.

"THE FLAYED ANGEL"

Gautier D'Agoty's mezzotint of the muscles of the back

Because her back is turned on us
and peeled outward from the ribs,
her namesake wings of skin surprise us
into thinking Fra Angelico—who taught
us all what textures wings might take
in two dimensions, an undulating
series of overlapping lines, a borrowing
from feathers, waves in sand, nothing
like the surface epidermis marked
with random blots or breathing glands
seeking after air any way they can.
If she were photograph or simple lines,
less art or more science, what we'd miss
is the man who had to be there
in the flesh with tray of graving tools
and pair of living eyes, who had
to read her with a knife and scrape
the burr from every rib, who had to know
the permanence of every cut. D'Agoty's
flaps of flesh are scored with etching's
textures, places where he meant the acid bath
to eat a weave of shadows into copper plates—
after which the inks pushed out their wells
of dark on water, thighs or fields, anywhere
the light is kept from falling, places
where the eye is urged to go but never see.

So this angel's wings have corrugations
like boxes, cups, or woven fabric,
a tidiness of purpose that belies the tease
of bundled curls caught above the collar
of her open spine in its red spindles
of gristle. The artist must have thought
the coif a kindness. Perhaps he even knew
that women in the countryside made ready
for a birth with combs and ribbons,
believed first pains meant time for curls.
So were these wings D'Agoty's kindness too,
his offer of a way she might escape
the grave? Or should we read these artful
cuts as consequence of process,
a simple accident of God.

CHERRIES

Rocked in my mother's pregnant amble,
and born into forty-five years in the dark,
the egg this child was also swayed in the arts
of lovers I took before you, fed with me

in the public markets of Baltimore and Denpasar
on oysters and rambutan, woke with me each year
to new waves of wander, fish and flower,
liqueur of each region, and bread of each village,

each cup of moonlight in the long sward
between my window and the Wannsee.
The egg he was heard the voices
of everyone I desired and held itself

in some deep hormonal bloom,
taking whatever was remarkable
in my life into its possibility.
We learned not to hurry in Balinese rain,

to listen for the rumble of wild boar
in the Malvan woods. We climbed
into planes bound for cities we'd never
visit again and skin we'd summon

with sobbing. And so, my husband,
as you dream of owning this child,
remember that he has ridden in my fire,
bathed in my blood, and sipped

at the breath I drew the first
time I saw what Rodin had clawed
from stone before he turned from Claudel
and went home for dinner and a clean shirt.

Remember that this child is collage
of everything before you, frangipani
and escargot, five-for-a-dollar boxes
of macaroni, and French cherries

from an old woman in Auvergne
who insisted on the gift
because it was so marvelous
to see a woman traveling alone.

WRITTEN ON THE SPINE

At the moment not a boat on the bay blue as the proverbial
bird egg, vague as a world beyond the scrim of a tear.

Thursday and tears, dear, can't be done. I always thought
hazel was a green, but air over water is also whiter at the edges
of its skirt sweep than air over prairie. What good would it do
to say *rapt*? Is it *rapture* or *raptor* I mean? I do have talons
and you the eyes muddied all of an evening over prawns
in lime.

Everything that disappears into you is lucky—apricot
cookies, that mango's swash below your plump lip,
purple as a girl's who's been pinching herself rich.

I'd cross the ChemLawn for sweet peas for you if you asked.
When the owners come home, there'll be a new alphabet
of hair in the pillows. Each reading the fine print on the other's
shins, they'll wonder whose hands those are making halos
above the heads of the pets.

We'll be the thousand dead
cells etched under their bones, answers to whole books
of evaporated questions in your backward scrawl on my spine.

Something might
that way be stashed for my travel, but not the roses dripping
their cups on the table, not the room bright with water
from below, the ferries scribbling toward islands.

I'm going to have to close my eyes after all, listening
for the crazy music of your slim feet, and then it's Bach
I'll want, all those violins skittering over the harpsichord's
club foot plunks.

                    No farewell then for the wicker chaise

with its appropriate arms, its plushy chat of pink peonies
under our knees. No farewell from the hot jaw
of the dishwasher which scoured the plates from which we fed,
and none from the giant black dog who learned in a day
to crave your hands dishing up pats and kibbles at five.

Let's say I'm the white pocket of air above the ferry
where gulls ride as if hung on wires. Let's say I'll be
that eddy of stillness above the push push of everything else.
And you,

             let's say you'll be the bird hanging on the string
of air I am, and you won't even have to breathe to move.

UP NORTH

I've had too much champagne, a sip
of cognac, a few blue hits on the good cigar
handed round at midnight in the blast
of bonfire on the frozen lake,

so we hurry back into our woods, drive
as far as the road is cleared, then toss
the bright plastic sled on the snow
where I lay me down to ride the last

half mile in. Prone, I see no more
than branches clasped above; cold pulls
its stilling finger along my spine,
and I hold my blood against it

to see what will push back. The snow
is deep but light, gives with shush
as I slip through, erase my lover's tracks.
He stops on hills, shifts his weight,

changes hands on the burning rope.
He's pulled in everything on sleds before,
wood, water, gear, boxes of wine and meat,
but never a woman, a weight that warms

the track and leaves a long gash of ice.
I brace my heels against the sled's hard rim,
the snow's chaff riding in around my thighs.
I know he wants this dark work of hauling me

to see if he can bear my weight, to dream me
as a stone, a corpse, pure sure thing.
And me, I'm not opposed to playing spoil
or chattel, allowing how he has to pull away

and lean against the dark to haul me up
hard against his heels. I let him have
the pleasure of dragging home his woman,
offer up my inert flesh as ballast, balance

against desire's dogged march into the dark.

SONNET ON THE INTERVAL DURING WHICH THE SUN IS BELOW THE HORIZON AT AN ANGLE LESS THAN ANY OF SEVERAL STANDARD ANGULAR DISTANCES

Comes a moment when a moment fears
its own blue shadow, and the windows
all deepen with purple curtains of more
shadow, and the little pens of the trees
against the stationary sky, doodle tiny springs
and circles on the dark. Then he tells me
we won't drink ever again, and the children
lean in like lilies crowded by shrubs,
and the breeze softens a little.
Somebody pops the cork anyway,
so the porch is a boat with giant masts
up into the dark where we sway for another
hour or two past the late anyway dusk,
holding our stems to the lights.

HYDROLOGIC SONNET

The earth, like a kicked heart, needs to warm
in increments, lest it glut our ten thousand bodies

of water, pour a winter's hale crust
south, thicken the tresses that halo

all the here, and dump muddy chronicles
through a whole continent's windy ribs,

those outpost attachments where we gathered
no moss and learned what the birds never did:

to stay in one place. This place, like the sensate
site we call simply *heart,* must allow its excesses

to transmute in mist, in fine strands of sweat,
in the attenuated wail of studied untouching.

This state, like cooled ardor, must pay back to the air
all those wan kisses in black slush and wishes.

OLD RADIO

An intelligence in a wilderness of boredom,
a luxury of syllables rolling like marbles
across the bare floor of those small-town years.

Oh, there was a body too, long and lean from days
of drinking dinner, the little pouch of belly
sliding under the ribs like an empty purse,

nothing to celebrate there, and an ordinary penis
less and less eager, but dutiful nonetheless to both
lover and wife. I was the former and glad to touch

what there was in exchange for the embroidery
of those sentences, long elegant borders with Victorian
spirals and gilded wings, half an hour before each

could come round to the bright spot
where it had been aimed from the start, yes,
all brocaded clauses and tasseled sofas of detail.

And what could be imagined: how agile that mind
might have been at twenty, before the years of steady
drink had stained the scrolled arms of the deepest

chairs, before the sadness dragged it like a mouse
crushed from the cat's jaw into my house
and left it as gift. Hypotactic silliness too,

the day I sold everything in the yard, and it sat
in the cheap screened house on the gold brocade sofa
nursing a scotch and pointing its toes at each other

like turtle doves. And all the hours I had of it
were a being in line for sentences that might unravel
into rivers of gist like the old radio in grandmother's

parlor with its pucker of static and knobs, or suddenly
give out a few bars of a song, a man's voice
slowing toward some grave import. Eloquence

with a bit of slouch, hips and hands. Cherubs
and angels in a fine verse of robes and clouds,
little specks of pink for mouths, the purple

of its articulation pouring toward me. I knew better
than to marry it, but I wanted to listen as long
as the Russian novel of it lasted. Now when it calls

once or twice in the year, no one here
can make out any words in the hum
of digital messaging, and I've married a man

who's all muscle and bluster, the thin high whine
of that old signal like unwritten lines
headed for Mars.

MIRABILIA, 1726

The local doctor took her for a "gloomy" sort,
a little daft, but strong. Her husband worked in cloth
and got on her three live young before this last,
most curious brood, a whole tribe of *Rabbets*
springing forth in groups of three or four.
Harvest in Godalming, Surrey, being nearly done,
and maybe that year only meager store,
leeks and turnips, a few thick-skinned gourds,
perhaps they'd been a little short, but rabbits
were abundant, and her boy able in getting
litters young and whole enough to plant
in Mary's lap, her roomy burrow readied
from easy passage of three prior infant
skulls. The village ready too for some miracle
of birth, even if it was just rabbits coming on
with winter's chill. By her own report, Mary took
a "longing" in the field one day, when a rabbit
sprang up like a bright idea from the dying
Queen Anne's lace and giant fennel,
so her five weeks' child afloat in the womb
fell away that night with a dream.
These blind and skinless babies curled
in the child's lost place and drank
of her waters, waited for light
and a man-midwife ready with belief.
Even after churching, more rabbits fell
from her marvelous loins in Guilford,
so the English Court brought her into town
to have a look, and though they caught

the serving boy with pockets full of blind
and slippery bunnies and trundled Mary Tofts
off to jail after her confession, the fact
remained that she had fooled at least
a half a dozen educated men by simply
being what she was, mammal, mystery,
cave and warren, unmapped womb,
a woman.

PREGNANT IN FLORENCE

Five months along, we shared a narrow bed
in Florence, and propped my burgeoned belly
on my hands, keeping us awake with all the need
my child had to breathe. But as we walked
the transepts and climbed into the icy crypts,
I searched the Virgin's unguarded face and marveled
at her countless marble hands curled around her child's
human genitals. Was she showing us the gateway
to his manly seed or holding off our view,
protecting what the artist wished to keep
apart, the male member fat and new?
I chose this city because I had a notion
that mothering was cause for celebration here,
and only now I learn what public spectacles
dissections were, staged in cool and spacious
churches, while artists, surgeons and the curious
crowded in to see the heart and horned uterus
lifted from the opened torsos of the criminal
and poor. I waddled into Dante's house
completely unaware of how death had held
its seminars just down the street, teaching
friends and enemies alike that the secret
of believing isn't simply seeing, but dwells
in cradling another, part by bloody part.

MANTRA OF THE BATH

This thing that has happened to you is for your
Instruction and your profit.

—Eagle to the Poet, Chaucer's
"The House of Fame"

His world was launched with *ball*
opened with *book*, days on end when he woke
murmuring *puppy, puppy* to the blind slugs
of his toes. I offer the little dainty of *love*,
but only hearty nouns get through.

He chatters at Pooh, whispers to water
raining through his lashes like nothing he can name.
When it clears, there is his tower of *turtles*
who've earned their epithets with being purple.

Still *love* won't gallop out of his glossary
of primary colors and plastic pets.
What could be said with those shining *balls*
or their matching yellow *hammer*?

I want him to have *book* and *duck* and *flower*,
but don't try *undoing, urchin, unguent.*

In the sizzle of my own milked neurons, *book*
connects *work, want, worlds*. But no lexicon
can tell how the world arrives in him. The history
of syllables is only comfort when we've lost

our stories for sounds. As surd and sonant
burble up from his new throat, they carry
his provisional signatures—all round fruits,
spots and buttons speak to us of *balls*—

and when he points to a swimming cherry
on a page and dubs it *fish,*
I could undo this world with *no,* wreck
his sweet conviction of a living fruit.

The mother tongue is a grave
and necessary unmaking,
so I settle for the marriage
of *cherry* and *fish,* for *love*

as the plastic noise of a toppling
tower of turtles.

ANAMNESIS, 1721–1740

> *Pain is inside the body. It leaves no trace for the*
> *historian unless complaints about it are recorded.*
>
> —Barbara Duden, *The Woman Beneath the*
> *Skin: A Doctor's Patients in Eighteenth-Century*
> *Germany*

After the French Revolution, the trend
in figuring anatomy was largely to dispense
with heads, and later still, the lexicon
of maladies began to pale, but Johann
Storch's sixteen hundred women
still have their tongues and readily report
a tearing in the jaw or rising in the throat.
This one has a cold womb, and that a womb fear,
another claims a squeezing in the heart.
Frights drive blood deep into the chest:
a mouse, a drunken spouse, fireworks
or children got with ghosts, an infant's
color, cough or trouble breathing.
Spleen fear, heart full of stilled wind,
stone colic, knots on the buttocks,
heat in the feet, fright in the limbs,
one shrunken breast or womb cramp
manifesting in the mouth. But anger
adheres to the stoutest heart, knocks
to get out, an urging in utero, a rattling
in the belly, stirring in the arm, breath
and speech flying out the ears, wind
turning toward the womb, an eating

in the breast, heavy tongue, flux, and fits
of the evil thing. Beyond which
whatever can't escape lives on
in the fisted heart of the child
and the child's child
as a big trouble with wind.

MOTHERHOOD AS PLACE

The house is a map the new mother unfolds
on her lap each day like a taxi driver
learning the routes. The avenue of love
becomes the park with the best playground.

The embassy of meals becomes a militarized
zone, the stove and cabinets
barricaded and closed to tourists.
But it's not enough that the rooms become

states, the furnishings friends or enemies;
Time that old thief, also steals
regularly away, so the room with the ugly
but safe stationary rocker swells with the hours

spent there, and the blue bears and bunnies
grow enormous in the light of synapse
and sway. The hallways are alleys where trash
erupts. The toilet a body of water she fears.

Suddenly, it all must be monitored, the opening
and closing of doors, the dryer, the temperature
of spoons, radiators, armpits,
what comes in on so many shoes,

the vicious world of worms always close
at hand. The poisonous dumb cane plant,
cold, September's first field mouse laying
his track of bacteria from door to door, books

that dream of falling from shelves, paper
that leaks cuts, the flailing hands of the child,
sharp little rags of his torn nails raking
the corners of his eyes. The house oppresses

even with so much light: interior walls
becoming spires and hedgerows—the exterior
world more and more exotic, simple grass
rare and lovely as the moon.

The child's damp jammies smell
of last night's dinner and this morning's shit,
green as the chewed leavings of a lawnmower
and somehow as fragrant. Crows stomp

on the roof, and as she looks down from the boy's
window onto the garden's eternal march and angle,
she thinks, Thank God for that white picket fence,
for the sturdy reality of so much apparently friendly cliché.

WEANING

I. Deer Season

The quiet of windows pours its sand in my ear.
What, what? ask the dolls of evening

though they do not wish to hear my answer.
Five hens are alive in the brush, purring

toward the slough. No one here has a rifle
but the wind turns abruptly and returns a report.

Three bright orange vests hang at the ready.
The doe turns in her frame above the stove,

and her season climbs like the moon into its place
in the sky's clock. The green theater

with its elegant aspens goes more threadbare
each week, so I'll soon see the others, heretofore

only heard. Just to the south the casino lights
ride the underbellies of clouds, and further

down the interstate more world twirls
in its papers and drinks, while the baby throws

his feet through the bars, and the father
takes him like a little canoe on the billowy

lake of his chest. Comes a mewling, then,
from my dark, a mooing, a whine, feathered

or furred I can't divine. The girl with the flat face
and bleached lips read her poems in crisp

Ivy League whatnot, but I got sidetracked
by the way her torso seemed stacked, pressed

in layers like shale, so there was a weight to her
that hung in the bottom of the eye like the bulk

of a tear that never quite falls. It's true
the intelligence was clear as green ice, and just

as hard, stripped of its *I* and heat. Her baby
burbled on in the back of the room happily not

in the poems. Oh little rabbit of grief on the spot
where the last dog was turned under, don't speak.

I make a fire, then dream a fire: wind carries
its gray rags into the woods, and the crackling

in the grate enters my ducts, wakes me.
When I look out, the grass along the fence

is crawling with light, and the last wild asters
press their blue buttons into the cold glass.

II. *The New Year*

Zero and a fine hard snow burns
when it hits bare skin. A white

ridge glows inside the birches
across the slough where snow articulates

the distance. Where water moves,
where the land heaves. I haul oak chunks

in a plastic sled. When I bend to stack
the splits, my breasts pop and burn,

and my child's face rises like a bird
razoring its shadow over the snow.

Wind takes the rag of some old self
and shakes it at me. The heart is only

another shape the view stretches to include.
Birches march out of the hardwoods

with their white waists radiant, so many
clones on one taproot. A jay circles

the full feeders fending off smaller birds.
I make this vocal gesture because self

is simply one edge of me. Out here
there's only an economy of wood burned

or to be burned, how much water's left
in the tank, how hard or soft the light.

Degrees and drafts. This room and everything in it
are mine, and though I try to be selfish and grim,

my child has made me enduringly plural,
more than I, but not quite we.

Black-capped chickadees flee
from three big jays at the feeder. Shrieking

and diving in the strong winter light, the jays
are not actually blue. Their feathers refract light

so they appear blue. Self-luminous,
hardy and belligerent as pronouns.

III. *Easter*

The kick of the screw finding purchase in pine
slams my wrist bone, elbow and shoulder,
but it's in, and the panel is up. Now another
and another until the wall is flush. I mark

and cut each length with the small tooth
of the new jigsaw my husband thought
I should have. Two days apart from him
and the child, I've forgotten the pump

to empty my breasts, so the saw's jump
at the end of the cut draws the burning
up. And with it a guilt as bright as the room
where I drive plank after plank against the studs,

each a satisfaction against the body's wish
to be elsewhere. Even into the night, I can't put
down my drill. I stoke the fire and drive
more screws, loving the growl when they're

in as far as they'll go. The mind arranging
which planks and trim tomorrow, next week
and spring. Even my sleep is a cutting and fastening
broken by my turning on the full globes

of my breasts. So toward morning I dream
of parties given by women I used to know,
and to which I'm not and will never be invited,
trays of fancy sandwiches and petit fours,

half moon glasses of seething champagne.

AIM

The palaeolithic bowman well knew where to find the heart of his victim, and he has portrayed it transfixed with arrows on the walls of his shelter.

—Charles Singer's account of the Western world's earliest anatomists, *A Short History of Anatomy*

Elmer Belt says Leonardo's drawings of the genital tracts
somehow failed to find their way with all the rest
to Windsor Castle's collection of the Queen.
These scrolls and doodles worked their way instead
to Weimar's Schlossmuseum, the German royals
making slightly less to-do over maps of genitalia
than Brits, but Elmer doesn't care to reproduce
Leonardo's most offensive image, man and woman
joined in coitus, their hips and thighs transparent,
so the penis gaining entry can be seen in its entirety,
their entrails coiled like vines of acorn squash,
while his substantial shaft aims for the open mouth
of her barracuda uterus. Though she has no bones
besides her half a spine, Leonardo's taken care to sketch
her lover's open eye tipped toward the empty space
of her missing face, which I imagine must, like Bernini's
naughty Saint Teresa, tip backward, eyes entirely closed
in legal ecstasy as the arrow points where we all know
God won't go. But Leonardo's man exudes a proper diffidence,
ample bonnet of curls whispering down the elegant
swirl of his tail as he throws one High Renaissance leg
over the mere suggestion of her thigh
and aims his animal spirit in.

THE HARRIERS

Memorial Day, 2004

Low over the swamp birch and sweet gale,
the broad torment of their shadows fall
on the marsh's invisible busy and small.
Snakes and shrews ride the roots, mice lurch
from one tussock to the next. The many
always fodder for the few, their tiny
pointed teeth useless in the sky.

Toothlessness lightens the harriers' skulls,
so they lift like foam, and belief wants to go
with them crisscrossing the marsh.
But the harriers, laying their hollow
bones on the wind, are only beautiful.
The male floats backward on the air
of his own arrival, passing his catch
to his mate in the sedge and gives me
one long look as he sits in the dead tree
at the edge of the marsh, curved, owlish head
cocked, funneling the small teedle-dee
of a distant rodent to its ear. *Harrier*
is from *harrow,* to torment, harass, assault,
also a cultivating implement set with spikes
for pulverizing soil. Significance falls apart
in my hands like a mist, though the harriers
have warm blood and four-chambered hearts.

The world they are offers no architecture
for an ethic: one dead language simply
rises through another, *raptor, rapture,*
and *rape,* for example, all sharing one
Latin root, *rapere, to seize.* The harriers
are only beautiful and will not be pressed

into resurrections. Even the highly significant
snake, hanging like a thread in the sky's white
neverending, knows the beetle in its belly isn't
his own and rides the talon of its captor,
who, when terror stands up and walks,
might be some kind of savior after all.

ANATOMY AT THE DINNER TABLE

Vesalius advises us to notice as we pluck
at table the cooked meat from the neck
of a calf, piglet or kid, the yellow ligament
so tough it's offered only to dogs.
The only ligament in the body unfit
for human consumption, it is offered
he says, in Brussels to young girls
because its pale yellow color is not
unlike the color they desire in their hair,
and the ligament itself diffuses its fine
strands into other parts of the body.
Not unusual then, to recommend
that one eat what one desires to wear
in the flesh, Beauty, we suppose,
being its own invitation to a meal.

ANATOMY OF THE UNSOUGHT FINDING

Throat and Acrobats: An Observational Study
Setting: University Hospital, Utrecht (two Saturdays, 1991)
Methods: Magnetic Resonance Imaging
Results: 11 slices of relatively good quality in 14 seconds
Conclusion: Such images are feasible and beautiful

What began as a hunch at a vision
of the throat's lobe mid-throb
with song, ended with a prone pair
of acrobats and new science
of love. When man is up
to his nuts in woman, he's bent
like a boomerang, and not,
as we so long thought, shooting
straight (Leonardo) or snaking
in an S (Dickinson—though how
he came to this conclusion using
unforgiving glass to play the male part,
I wouldn't like to guess). One third
of man's root participates, and woman's
innermost parts are busy making room,
her anterior vaginal walls "tenting"
when she's ready. But the new news
is old after all: that Hippocrates
was partly right: the uterus moves
when woman is aroused, ascending
even before he enters in, carrying
its expansive cavity of possibilities
safely north, even though the only

couple in the study able to cavort
and climax under observation
were acrobats, adept at being prone,
spilling stillness, or turning up
a bit of serendipity on cue.

PAROUS IN PARIS

Grief whittles away at the last of my maternal
fat as I cross the Seine in feeble autumn light
to present myself for rendezvous
with Monsieur Director, *Institut d'Anatomie.*
Only to wait the requisite four French hours
for him to show: my thinned skin zinging
with each squeal of the secretary who rifles
invoices (for God knows what) and flirts
with a man lolling about in scrubs,
his knuckles blue and chapped from his work
in the fridge. But it's this man who later reads
my grief as the small thing it will one day be
when we join him in the cadaver room
where he sings and slings cold heads
from bin to shelf for dental students
to unclench. I've left my only child
home in another country for this walk
into a history of the body of woman
in labor, so all four hours I kill
waiting in the unforgiving chair,
the coppery scent of formaldehyde
sticking in my throat, I fight down
the unthinkable news delivered
at dawn via e-mail: someone else
is in my marriage bed, her broad thighs
loading up on genes, the very same
that give my son his dazzle and dash,
his own sweet power to sunder.

HOMAGE TO A TESTORE BASS

stalk:

If this were landscape, what would it be?
Bluff and hollow? Beach and dune?
A place where the stones are round,
and the curve of a cape turns its hip
and rump to the sea? Or mountains
brought to their knees by an inland lake.
Any of these edged with hills where wheat
whispers itself toward ripeness.

torso:

She could hear his weight and muscle, the hum
and double of him in the seamed dark body
of the bass, but it was only in the confluence
of the seen and the heard at heart
that she was stricken with want.

bread:

He liked to play in the kitchen
where sound fell around him most rightly,
and there, barefoot and robed, he turned
the gold pegs and drew long notes,
mixed sound and scent: toast, dust, and love,
varnish and vanishings, the lacquered rib
pressed to his bare knee, the back of its neck
sliding over his palm; drawing demons

and dreams from the realm of the seen
to the heard.

doll:

Its shoulders, like his, slope — the right
more deeply than the left — and inside,
there's a good void that loves its own hum,
patterned light, and a tiny post that pays
the sound back to the player's thigh.

It's a body better than ours, palpable, a challenge
to the mortal and perfect in proportion;
it understands nothing but touch,
as does he who plays it.

boat:

Monumental shape cloaked and leaning
in the kitchen's corner, it goes nowhere
without a body and a map. Invites us to cleave
each to the other lest we drown. It teaches
the image to marry the note, the silence
to bathe in a sequence of sounds.

Who draws music from such a shape, draws also
my heart in the great varnished boat
that creaks and drifts toward the end
of a concerto, an hour, a life.

torso again:

Cremonese violin makers love the bulk
of the seated female nude: the shape we know
as "hour-glass," they know from the back as craft;
each carves nightly the two dark f-holes
just above his lover's ample hips.

Somewhere between wood and breath,
belly of spruce, broad maple back
her scroll above him bows in prayer.

carafe:

Listen: three hundred years of disquieted hours,
secrets freed from those who kept them,
illicit couplings, cities powdered in war;
pettiness and paltry tunes, crushing tenderness,
a varnish the color of claret once, and hands
that drew whole groves of bows,
sometimes those who understood
nothing about the heart except that it hurt.

cherries:

Made and broken and remade before we were born,
we see it in pieces, its unvarnished heart exposed
in a Cremona shop. Or on a stage, Milano's La Scala,
Barolo's little church. In a player's kitchen,

his breakfast, like ours, spread on the table,
bread, jam of summer's cherries lighting up
the cutlery, a woman standing by
in love at once with the man and what stands
between; they open her with the weight
of both blood and beauty on the eye,
what they make of the flesh
in the mind's ear.

bees:

Tiny canyons worn in the tips
of his fingers where a river of string
has worn its way through Brahms and Bach,
He's barefoot and ripe against the body
of the bass, 300 years of sweet dying
in the hive under his thumb.

torso, the last:

His wrists are permanently tipped, the left
to rest the amber neck in the place where the varnish
is gone, the right at an angle that bears down
on the strings like a mouth, and under his arm
there's a soft place where he hugs the slope.

It takes its place among the tuxes and silk,
the strict lips of the oboist on her brittle reeds,
the long wings of the trombones sliding to

and away, the timpanist with his ear to the skin,
stilling it with his finger pads, horns dumping
their bells of spit while they wait for the flutes
to finish.

doll again:

We'll always carry it with us, this extra body
from an old world, at once sexual and immortal,
it has the shape of my hips and the strength
of his thighs. Who dreamed such a shape
that when I first saw him touching it,
I also had to be touched?

We've driven north and west with the Testore
silenced and swaddled between us.
Among suitcases and bedrolls, remnants
of a picnic, its elegant scroll yokes us
and points our way home.

BRIDAL WEAR

The aisles of frocks whitecap on their racks,
and I want someone to go in for me, find
the one without beads, sequins, blisters of lace.
I can't abide the leagues of white, thickets of silk

and tulle, sateen gloves, baskets wrapped in net and puff.
I swoon with headache from the sickened store air,
the gowns gassed in truckloads before they left
Malaysia or Taiwan. Imposter in the bridal *shoppe*,

I'm middle-aged, doubtful, even appalled by the project,
but here nonetheless, looking, like everyone else,
for the perfect fog of organdy or taffeta in which
to meet the lover I want to be my last. I drop

the bargain dress over my head in a hall of mirrors
that rivals Versailles, step up on the block
and float my image in champagne satin,
ashamed I've even found one dress to want.

The price tags flutter and beckon. The beadwork
loosens and ticks as I twirl. But everyone around me
donning gowns grows more beautiful, impossible
to miss: giant bleached insects with their cinched waists

and bubbled breasts, wads of train fizzing behind them.
Outside it's a September afternoon, one of the last
warm days, slow bees beading the muggy air,
an afternoon when I ought to be in a canoe

with my lover, sequins of river light spreading out
behind us, a bottle of wine in the dry sack,
my oar dipped in the slowed autumn current
of the Cannon, and behind me, my intended

dipping with me, so we move together as if
down an aisle, though with the peace
of perfect assurance that where we're headed
matters much less than where we are.

OUTLIVING THE LYRIC MOMENT

> *Angel and muse escape with violin and compass;*
> *the duende wounds.*
>
> —*Federico García Lorca*

I didn't expect to escape. I've stepped out of planes
into Madrid and Bangkok, Prague and Seoul,
each time a solo in a world that was, if not cruel,
supremely indifferent to the fact of my breath.

I loved where I could, did not imagine my mouth
without light, fish at home in my bluest wells.
I went in a stalk of pure wanting that knows
there's no getting, and collected tiny lemons

of joy when they ripened in reach of a window
in Vence where I happened also on tangles
of grapes fallen and trodden on the road to the sea.
I plucked green stones from Spanish sand, wore

the white hibiscus for a day behind my ear
where it softened with rot in a pattern of etch.
In Andalusia the wine is new and ruby, breath
and aroma the tools of being in places where days

are paid out like so many queens on obsolete
coins. Now, not suddenly, but after long balance
of what there is against what might or might never be,
the never-was has dared to love me back.

So it was death all along who stood in the ferry
with his dirty blond hair and bright nylon pack,
but I never imagined he'd be so young
as he slung the pack, leapt to the shore

and never looked back for me. That's why
my flesh loves me today. There are salt and heat
and a body of bread, new if not endless, and a rumor
if not news of the future. It dies as it lived, the idea

of duende, a proximity, a song we don't necessarily
need in a land of snow and icy green lakes where
the weather's a tomb and the lover's strong thigh
is white and marvelous as marble, a throne

on which I suppose I could sit and grow handsomely old.

NOTES

Cover Illustration and "Gautier D'Agoty's Écorchés"

Courtesy of the National Library of Medicine's "Dream Anatomy" exhibit. Jacques Fabien Gautier D'Agoty, artist and printer, *Anatomie des parties de la génération de l'homme et de femme. Paris, 1773. Colored mezzotint.*

Jacques Fabien Gautier D'Agoty (1711-85) artist, engraver, printer and publisher of anatomical illustrations using the mezzotint method invented by Le Blon. His figures were sometimes life sized or done in fold-out pages and elaborately colored. Roberts and Tomilson in *The Fabric of the Body* characterize his prints thusly: "Gautier's pictures seem to us to be in the tradition of the early gravida illustrations . . . often attracting attention through sexual emphasis: dissected parts were placed within a 'living' body, usually possessing a lively face, whose expression is sometimes quizzical, sometimes serene, always with a romantic and elegant hair-style." (524)

"Rough Music, Edinburgh, 1829"

The story of prostitute Mary Paterson's murder and sixteen others in Edinburgh by William Burke and Hare, and the anatomist Robert Knox who bought the corpses of the sixteen murder victims from Burke and Hare, is recounted slightly differently in a variety of sources. I rely, for my factual details, on the accounts in Ruth Richardson's *Death, Dissection and the Destitute* and Roberts and Tomlinson's *The Fabric of the Body: European Traditions of Anatomical Illustration.*

Rough Music cited in Richardson as part of a "skimmington," a tradition of public protest in Scotland, and "mode of expressing public disquiet, and of obtaining popular justice. It would usually be mounted publicly to shame transgressors of implicit social codes—in cases of wifebeating, flagrant marital infidelity, or of over-speedy remarriage by widows or widowers . . . a composite custom, generally featuring one or more of the following elements: . . . 'rough music'—a cacophony of sound . . . some sort of processional progress, and could feature a symbolic figure at its focus—an effigy—the burning of which was usually the climax of the event."

"Mother and Son"

LEGO is from the Danish *Leg Godt*, meaning "play well," or in Latin, "I put together."

"Wandering Uterus"

"It was a common notion of medieval times that the uterus was subdivided into seven cells. The idea was popularized by the widely read *Liber physiognomiae* or *De secretis naturae* of Michael Scot, one of the founders of Latin Averroism." (O'Malley and Saunders, p. 464, *Leonardo da Vinci on the Human Body: The Anatomical, Physiological and Emryological Drawings of Leonardo da Vinci*.)

"Map of the Interior"

The penultimate ten lines of this poem are taken verbatim from Charles Singer's *A Short History of Anatomy from the Greeks to Harvey*, 1925, page 115.

"On the Vulva" and "figure 99"

Figure numbers in both poems refer to notes and figures of the corresponding numbers in Robert Latou Dickinson, *Atlas of Human Sex Anatomy: A Topographical Hand Atlas*. "figure 99" consists verbatim of the notes for *figure 99*.

"The wrinkles or folds of the vulva have indicated to us the position of the gate-keeper of the castle which is always found where the meeting of the longitudinal wrinkles occurs." (Leonardo da Vinci, notes on plate 200 in O'Malley and Saunders, 1952)

"Recipe for Couples Therapy"

"Dislocation of the Womb" (Hippocrates, *Nature of Women* 8, 3+Vii 322-4, trans. Littre): "When her womb moves toward her liver, she suddenly loses her voice and her teeth chatter and her colouring turns dark. This condition can occur suddenly, while she is in good health. . . . When this condition occurs, push your hand down below her liver, and tie a bandage below her ribs. Open her mouth and pour in very sweet-scented wine; put applications on her nostrils and burn foul-scented vapours below her womb . . ."

"Venus Endormi"

These five models are housed in the Delmas-Orfila-Rouvière Museum in Paris. In addition to the so-called *Venus Endormi*, there are four additional life-sized models representing normal childbirth, childbirth with the assistance of forceps, unsuccessful labor after which the fetus must be removed part by part with hooks, and a cesarean birth.

"The Resurrection Trade"

Anatomie des parties de la génération de l'homme, et de la femme, représentées avec leurs couleurs naturelles, selon le nouvel art, joints à l'Angéologie de tout le corps humain, et à ce qui concerne la grossesse et les accouchemens. Par M. Gautier Dagoty pére, Anatomiste pensionné du Roi. Paris, chez J.B. Brunet et Deomonville, 1773, fol., 8 plates. The edition to which these plate numbers refer is housed in the *Bibliothèque de l'Académie Nationale de Médecine,* Paris.

"These eight plates can be put together into four figures: a male body, a female body, a pregnant woman, and a woman in labor. None of these figures are life-sized." *History and Bibliography of Anatomic Illustration,* Ludwig Choulant, trans., Frank Mortimer, 1852, Leipzign Rudolph Weigel.

"Torso of a Woman Gone with Child, 1774"

Jan Van Rymsdyck (also sometimes spelled Riemsdyk): Illustrator for three important anatomists from 1750-84, Hunter, Smellie and Jenty. The original of the two drawings (with book in front of the vagina) is in the Hunterian Collection, Glasgow (Az.1.4) and reprinted in Helen King's *Hippocrates' Women: Reading the Female Body in Ancient Greece,* 1998. In the published version of Hunter's anatomy, the book has been removed.

"*Madame du Coudray's Woman Machine, 1756*"

All of the factual details for this poem can be found in Nina Rattner Gelbart's *The King's Midwife: A History and Mystery of Madame du Coudray*.

"'*The Flayed Angel*'"

The name by which the image of D'Agoty's illustration of the muscles of the back from *Myologie complete en couleur et grandeur naturelle, compose del'Essai et de la Suite de l'Essai d'anatomie en tableux imprimés* is generally known.

"*Mirabilia, 1726*"

Details for this poem, factual and fabulous, come from the account in Jacques Gélis' *History of Childbirth: Fertility, Pregnancy and Birth in Early Modern Europe*.

"*Anamnesis, 1721–1740*"

Johann Storch, 1681-1752?, author of *Diseases of Women*, an eight volume work, seven of which are devoted to case studies of women he attended from approximately 1721-1740. There are over 1,800 cases of 1,650 different women, all written in the vernacular rather than in Latin, the medical language of the day. According to Barbara Duden (60), "Storch himself listed the following as factors for the success of his practice: 'divine providence' and his skill in 'women's cures,' to which his own wife was walking testimony, for, as he dryly remarked, 'divine dispensation has given me a woman from whom I could learn more than from hundreds of other patients. For up to her sixty-first year she was laid up fifteen times with this disease [pleuritic fever], eight times she survived illness in childbed, twice she had cold fever and jaundice, she often suffered from hemorrhoids, ten years she spent complaining about stones, not to mention other inherited hysterical misfortunes." (Duden quotes from Storch's autobiography, 16)

"Aim"

Elmer Belt, author of *Leonardo the Anatomist.*

"Anatomy at the Dinner Table"

"It will be possible to learn the nature of this ligament whenever the neck of a calf, piglet, kid, or even a more mature steer is put on the dinner table. This is the ligament, the yellow body, that is rejected as unfit for consumption. Because of its toughness, the people of Brussels call it uvas, and they recommend girls eat it to promote the growth of hair, making fun of them, I believe, because it is separated like hair into the other parts of the body and because of its pale yellow color." Andreas Vesalius, *De Humani Corporis Fabrica, Book II, Chapter 40.*

"Anatomy of the Unsought Finding"

The experiment and article to which this poem refers: "Magnetic resonance imaging of male and female genitals during coitus and female sexual arousal," Willibrord Weijmar Schultz, *British Medical Journal,* December 18, 1999; 319:1596–1600. The description of the study's images as "feasible and beautiful" is taken directly from the article's "conclusion." The title is taken from another article by one of this study's instigators, Pek Van Andel, "Anatomy of the unsought finding: Serendipity: origin, history, domains, traditions, appearances and programmability. *British Journal Phil Sci* 1994; 45:631–648. Van Andel "does not want to be acknowledged for his idea of using MRI to study coitus. He excuses himself by quoting the French romantic poet Alphonse de Lamartine (1700-1869): *C'est singulier! Moi, je pense jamais, mes idles pensent pour moi."*

"Homage to a Testore Bass"

Carlo Antonio Testore (1693–1765), Italian maker of fine string instruments, known particularly for his double basses.

WORKS CITED AND CONSULTED

Adams, J.N. *The Latin Sexual Vocabulary.* Baltimore: The Johns Hopkins University Press, 1982.

Angier, Natalie. *Woman: An Intimate Geography.* New York: Anchor, 1999.

Aries, Philippe. *The Hour of Our Death.* New York: Vintage, 1981.

Belt, Elmer. *Leonardo the Anatomist.* New York: Greenwood Press, 1955.

Blumenfeld-Kosinski, Renate. *Not of Woman Born: Representations of Caesarean Birth in Medieval and Renaissance Culture.* Ithaca: Cornell University Press, 1990.

Bouce, P. G. *Sexuality in Eighteenth Century Britain.* Manchester, 1982.

Bynum, W.F. and Porter, R. *William Hunter and the Eighteenth-Century Medical World.* Cambridge: Cambridge University Press, 1985.

Carlino, Andrea (trans. John Tedeschi and Anne C. Tedeschi). *Books of the Body: Anatomical Ritual and Renaissance Learning.* Chicago: University of Chicago Press, 1999.

Charlton, D.G. *Secular Religions in France 1815–1879.* London, 1963.

Choulant, Ludwig and M. Frank. *History and Bibliography of Anatomic Illustration* Cambridge, reprint edition, 1993.

Corbin, Alain (trans. Miriam Kochan). *The Foul and the Fragrant: Odor and the French Social Imagination.* Cambridge: Harvard University Press, 1986.

Dickinson, Robert Latou. *Atlas of Human Sex Anatomy: A Topographical Hand Atlas.* Huntington, New York: Krieger Publishing, 1949.

Duden, Barbara (trans. Thomas Dunlap). *The Woman Beneath the Skin: A Doctor's Patients in Eighteenth-Century Germany.* Cambridge: Harvard University Press, 1991.

Ehrenreich, B. and English, D. *For Her Own Good: 150 Years of the Experts' Advice to Women.* New York, Anchor 1978.

Gelbart, Nina Rattner. *The King's Midwife: A History and Mystery of Madame du Coudray.* Berkeley: University of California Press, 1998.

Gélis, Jacques (trans. Rosemary Morris). *History of Childbirth: Fertility, Pregnancy and Birth in Early Modern Europe.* Boston: Northeastern University Press, 1991.

Jordanova, Ludmilla. "Gender, Generation, and Science: William Hunter's Obstetrical Atlas," in *William Hunter and the Eighteenth-*

Century Medical World, ed. W. F. Bynum and Roy Porter (Cambridge: Cambridge University Press, 1985), pp. 385–412.

Jordanova, Ludmilla. *Sexual Visions: Images of Gender in Science and Medicine between the Eighteenth and Twentieth Centuries*. Madison: University of Wisconsin Press, 1989.

Keller, E.F. *Reflections on Gender and Science*. New Haven: Yale University Press, 1985.

Kemp, M. *Dr. William Hunter at the Royal Academy of Arts*. Glasgow: Glasgow University Press, 1975.

King, Helen. *Hippocrates' Woman: Reading the Female Body in Ancient Greece*. London: Routledge, 1998.

Leavitt, J.W. *Brought to Bed: Childbearing in America 1750-1950*. Oxford: Oxford University Press, 1986.

Martin, Emily. *The Woman in the Body: A Cultural Analysis of Reproduction*. Boston: Beacon Press, 1987.

O'Malley, Charles and Saunders, J.B. *Leonardo da Vinci on the Human Body: The Anatomical, Physiological and Emryological Drawings of Leonardo da Vinci*. New York: Gramercy, 2003.

Porter, Roy, ed. *Patients and Practitioners: Lay Perceptions of Medicine in Pre-Industrial Society*. Cambridge: Cambridge University Press, 1986.

Roberts, K.B. and J.D.W. Tomlinson. *The Fabric of the Body: European Traditions of Anatomical Illustrations*. Oxford: Oxford University Press, 1992.

Rousseau, G.S. and Porter, R. eds. *Sexual Underworlds of the Enlightenment*. Manchester: Manchester Universitiy Press, 1988.

Schultz, Bernard. *Art and Anatomy in Renaissance Italy*. Ann Arbor: University of Michigan, 1985.

Sims, Michael. *Adam's Navel: A Natural and Cultural History of the Human Form*. New York: Viking, 2003.

Sussman, G. *Selling Mothers' Milk: The Wet-Nursing Business in France, 1715-1914*. Urbana: University of Illinois Press, 1982.

Thornton, John L. *Jan van Rymsdik: Medical Artist of the Eighteenth Century*. Cambridge: Oleander Press, 1981.

Wilson, Adrian. *The Making of Man-Midwifery: Childbirth in England, 1660–1770*. Cambridge: Harvard University Press, 1995.

Leslie Adrienne Miller is the author of four previous poetry collections: *Eat Quite Everything You See, Yesterday Had a Man in It, Ungodliness*, and *Staying Up for Love*. She teaches at the University of Saint Thomas in Saint Paul, Minnesota.

The Resurrection Trade has been set in Bembo, a typeface produced by Monotype in 1929 and based on a roman cut in Venice by Francesco Griffo in 1495. Book design by Wendy Holdman. Composition at Prism Publishing Center, Minneapolis, Minnesota. Manufactured by Versa Press on acid-free paper.